W9-DCY-355

CAPE BRETON
Island of Islands

CAPE BRETON
Island of Islands

Photographed by
Warren Gordon
Foreword by
Kenzie MacNeil and Max MacDonald

Steel Town Publishing

To the memory of my father, Edward Gordon, a true Cape Breton pioneer and friend to all.

With special thanks to my friend Sherman Hines, Master and Fellow of Photographic Arts.

Gordon Photographic Ltd.
367 Charlotte St.
Sydney, N.S.
B1P 1E1

Canadian Cataloguing in Publication Data

Gordon, Warren 1951 -

Cape Breton Island of Islands

ISBN 0-9690395-1-4

1. Cape Breton Island, N.S. — Description and travel — Views. 1. Title

Printed and bound in Hong Kong by
Scanner Art Services Inc. Toronto

Production Artwork by B. Koo & Associates
Toronto, Ontario, Canada

Foreword

Island of Islands!

To anyone who has never crossed the Canso Causeway or experienced Cape Breton Island in any other way, that may seem to be an arrogant claim. But to any and all who have lived and breathed "Cape Breton", it's an unerring truth - a fact which is felt.

Here is an Island formed by the passing of glaciers, the shift of continents, the ebb and flow of tide and the wearing and healing of water. There it stands among the revolutions of the earth and the stream of time - a rock.

Cape Breton defies definition. As the flower eludes understanding when its petals are pulled apart, so the Island refuses to be fully explained. To the touch, the smell, the sound, the taste and to the view it is very real - but to the sixth sense, the one which stirs the heart and soul, there is contrast and contradiction, paradox and irony and above all, mystery.

The ever-present water of Cape Breton - its streams and rivers, lakes and ocean - will at one time lull you to profound peace and at another bring you to your knees in humility, in awe and reverence. The land - the hills and mountains, valleys and glens, coast fronts and beaches - ranges from pastoral serenity on one hand to striking and powerful majesty on the other.

The seasons affect the Island with an incredible array of weather - crossing the spectrum from a soft, warm summer breeze to a white and wild snow storm. The weather from the Gulf of St. Lawrence on the Island's west coast can be completely different from that of the Cabot Strait on the northeastern shore. It may be sunny and clear in the industrial eastern side while fog and rain daunt the south and southwestern coast. The Bras d'Or Lakes have unique patterns of their own. There is so much variety in the weather, that it occupies a good deal of our conversation.

The irony to all this purifying nature is provided, of course, by human nature. The serene horizons are broken by the stacks and towers of industry - pulp and paper, steel and coal, coal-fired power and nuclear water - and by the people who built them.

Cape Bretoners themselves defy definition - so much so that we spend a fair amount of time trying to figure each other out. "What's your father's name?" is a common and serious question. These are people who are literally from all over the world. The Highland Scots make up the majority but are balanced by Acadians and Irish English and Micmac, Slavs and Europeans, Asians and Africans (via the West Indies). The cultural variety of these backgrounds is still greatly respected but in the passage of two hundred years of Cape Breton's history the bloodlines have blurred and blended to create the Cape Bretoner.

No stranger to hard work and hard times, to absentee control over industry and politics and to forced exodus from the Island when the limits of industry and politics require, the Cape Bretoner is still a Cape Bretoner. Whether an exile in the Alberta Tarsands, the offshore oil rigs, the central North American auto plants, New England or California, the longing for "home" is maintained. And for those who managed to stay, the shared bond with those abroad is a deep and heartfelt love of the Island - as magical and mysterious as the Island itself.

Responding to the success of "Images of Cape Breton", Warren Gordon continues to celebrate that love for the Island in this, his second book. He adheres to his unique format of blending photographic and poetic imagery. Warren's use of song lyrics from a number of Island writers along with his photographs, invites the viewer to hear the peal of the violins and the passion of the songs; to more fully feel the intensity of Cape Breton. Warren's is a positive point of view - one for the memories of Cape Bretoners and visitors alike and one from his heart for this Island of Islands.

Kenzie MacNeil
Max MacDonald
November 1984

Near Lake Ainslie

Late spring, the trees have turned green,
There's sheep on the hills, and birds on the wing;
Over my shoulder the last time I'm seeing
The old house, all weathered and grey.

We talked 'till three, my father and me
And the fiddle tunes flowed like the clear Margaree.
"Never forget who you are, son," said he,
As I followed my brothers away.

One thing I know, wherever I go
My heart's in Cape Breton — it will always be so.
Whenever a fiddler rosins the bow
My first and last thoughts are of home.

Alistair D. MacDonald

Fourchu

Overleaf: Iona

C. MONTY MacMILLAN

Blacksmith, Highland Village, Iona

Highland Village, Iona

Far from the scenes of childhood days
It was my lot to roam
Across the sea to a foreign land,
Far from my Highland home.
In dreams I saw the village
Where my sad heart longed to be -
Where the waters of Iona rippled
Down to the deep, blue sea.

Lillian Crewe Walsh

Spinner, Highland Village, Iona

Milling Frolic, Catalone

Anns a' gheamhradh, am an fhuachd,
Am nam bainnsean, am nan luadh;
Chluinnte gillean air cleith-luaidgh,
'S gruagaich' le guth cruaidgh 'g an leantainn.

Nuair bhiodh am fùcadh ullamh, réidh,
Chuirt' an fhidheall sin air ghleus;
Dhannsamaid air ùrlar réidh,
Gur e "Cabar Féidh" bu mhath leinn.

In winter, the season of cold,
In the season of weddings and milling frolics,
Young men could be heard at the milling-board;
The girls' clear voices would follow their lead.

And when the milling was finished,
The fiddle then would be tuned,
And we would dance on the smooth, bare floor;
"Cabar Féidh" was our favourite tune.

Dan Alex MacDonald

Fiddlers, St. Ann's

The Island is ready, the hands are all clasped,
The footsteps are shuffling, the fiddlers are asked
To play all that they know with their hearts and their souls,
So we'll rise above, rise above Folly.

Kenzie MacNeil

Gaelic College, St. Ann's

Baddeck

Beinn Bhreagh, summer home of Alexander Graham Bell

Far on Beinn Bhreagh's side wander the lost lambies.
Here, there and ev'rywhere, ev'rywhere their troubled mammies
Find them and fold them deep, fold them to sleep singing:
  Caidil gu law, laddie, law, laddie,
  Sleep the moon away.

Kenneth Leslie

Margaree River

East Margaree

On an evergreen-treed mountain,
There awaits a world to see -
Here to come and watch in wonder
On a bended knee -
Looking down the quiet valley,
Cradled by some sloping hills -
Quiet save the sound of water
Running, running where it wills.

Kenzie MacNeil

St. John's United Church, Inverness

Inverness

In a small, quiet village
That stands by the sea,
I played with my comrades,
Light-hearted and free;
Some sleep in the churchyard,
While others have roamed
And left far behind them
Their Cape Breton Home.

Lillian Crewe Walsh

Whale Cove

In the wind, the gentle wind,
The eagles circle higher;
While down below the songbirds sing
Their voices never tire.
And on the wave, the rolling wave,
The tempting ocean calling,
Heaving up all those who brave her,
Cresting and then falling.

Kenzie MacNeil

Cabot Trail

Overleaf: Cheticamp

REPAS MEALS
ACADIEN
MUSEUM
&
HANDCRAFTS

St. Joseph Du Moine

La pêche sera bonne,
Amis, partons sans bruits;
La pleine lune donne
Presque toute la nuit.
Il faut qu'avant l'aurore
Nous soyons de retour,
Pour admirer encore
Les merveilles du jour.

Partons, la mer est belle;
Embarquons nous, pêcheurs.
Guidons notre nacelle,
Ramons avec ardeur.
Aux mats hisons les voiles.
Le ciel est pur et beau;
Je vois briller l'étoile
Qui guide les matelots.

traditional

Les Trois Pignons, Cheticamp

Nicolas Denys Museum, St. Peters

Fortress Louisbourg

Gabarus

Gabarus

L'Ardoise

Point Michaud

Maybe go walkin' the woods and the shore,
Maybe have someone with me.
There's no need for talk, lyin' on a flat rock,
Watchin' the sun kiss the sea.

Leon Dubinsky

Petit De Grat

Lady of the Assumption Church, Arichat

Little River

Little River

Cast your nets on these waters, your line on the sea,
Your sights on horizons wherever you please,
For together we'll weather the tide that prevails
With the sun on our shoulders, the wind in our sails.

Allister MacGillivray

Ingonish

Cape Smoky's winding stairway
   Overlooks the rolling sea,
And the quiet Ingonishes
   Lie in shelter 'neath its lee;

In their dreams, thy wandering children
   See again thy hills and dales,
and Their hearts come o'er the waters
   When it's twilight on the Trail.

Lillian Crewe Walsh

Ingonish

Overleaf: Keltic Lodge, Ingonish

Lone Shieling

Whether the blood be Highland, Lowland or no,
And whether the skin be black or white as the snow,
Of kith and of kin we're one, be it right, be it wrong -
As long as our voices join this chorus of song.

traditional

Near the Lone Shieling

Beulach Ban Falls

Mabou Harbour

Mabou

Where the trees of Cape Mabou are kissed by the sky.
They wander, yes, wander, they wonder why.
In their fashion they sing of my passion,
For their home is my home - why should I roam?

The sun-setting sky that glitters the deep
Warms and comforts the grazing sheep.
The bell from the Chapel is beckoning me,
Gathering past times down by the salt sea.

Annie Mae MacPherson-Skinner

St. Joseph Du Moine

Pleasant Bay

Gillis' Falls

Englishtown

Englishtown Ferry

When the moon goes down in Englishtown
And the morning comes to call,
When it's still supposed to be summer
And you know what follows fall,
I will raise my cup when the sun comes up
To another day that's new -
I am honoured sharing life with you.

Leon Dubinsky

Black Brook

Sunrise Valley

But in a wild and raging wind,
When peace is bent and we must bend,
Hold harmony in memory
Then song will be your friend;
For in the heart, the joyful heart,
There'll you'll find no reason
But love of friendship, love of life,
Land and sea and season.

Kenzie MacNeil

Overleaf: Big Intervale

North Mountain

Middle River

North Bay, Ingonish

Wreck Cove

Marion Bridge

Pierce Peters with his team, Mira Road

Wentworth Park, Sydney

All the tourists are gone - it's December in Sydney;
Think I'll go to the park and see the ducks that can't fly.
When the ice it comes in, they'll all migrate to Westmount
And I'll turn my heat up and move on inside.

I'm in Sydney and it's the middle of winter;
You could freeze from your nose to your toes,
So keep your back to the storm
And keep your skates at the Forum,
And I'll see you in June when it's warm.

Ronald MacEachern

Great Bras d'Or Channel

Low Point

Main-A-Dieu

Blessing of the fleet, Main-A-Dieu

Green Cove

Overleaf: Nova Scotia Forest Industries, Port Hawksbury

It's a working man I am
And I've been down underground
And I swear to God if I ever see the sun
Or for any length of time I can hold it in my mind
I never again will go down underground.

Rita MacNeil

Hot saw cutting rails, Sysco

Children still play in the factory town,
The engineer waves on his way down the line,
Bloodlines run deep in the factory town,
Mamma says "Boy, just give it time."

A test of mettle for the boys at the open hearth,
A test of mettle, luck and skill,
A test of mettle for the ones left behind,
A test of mettle down at the mill.

Max MacDonald

Tapping an Open Hearth Furnace, Sysco

East Bay

Inverness

And it must be something
To rise at the dawn,
You travel the roads
And you're all alone -
Oh, old man, what have they done to you?
And the tools of your trade
You hold in your hands;
You had your life
And you lived it well,
And the mark of your craft
Can be found in the past dwellings
That you made.

Rita MacNeil

Kruzenshtern, USSR
The Tall Ships, July 7 to 11, 1984, Sydney

Men that are born to the ocean
  On the land are never free;
The sea is their rightful heritage
  And their hearts belong to the sea.

Lillian Crewe Walsh

Kruzenshtern, USSR

Sagres II, Portugal

Dar Mlodziezy, Poland

Gorch Fock, Germany

Glace Bay Harbour

Small craft in a harbour that's still and serene
Give no indication what their way has been,
They rock at their moorings, all nestled in dreams,
Away from the roll of the sea.

Their stern lines are groaning a lullaby air,
A ghost in the cuddy, a gull on the spar;
But never they whisper of journeys afar -
Away from the roll of the sea.

Oh, had they the tongues for to speak,
What tales of adventure they'd weave,
But now they are anchored to sleep
And slumber alee.

Allister MacGillivray

North Sydney

Cossit House

Town Crier, Sydney

Overleaf: Wentworth Park and Area

Neil's Harbour

I hear the ocean as it runs on the shore,
I see an old friend comin' in through the door,
I taste the salt of the spray on my face,
I feel my heartbeat for that one special place.

I'm home in my habour at the edge of the sea
And when we are parted, she calls out to me:
"Come home again, lover, won't you come home to me,
Home in your harbour at the edge of the sea..."

Leon Dubinsky

Cabot Trail

Mira River

Island of islands, farewell has come;
time must have its way.
Island of islands, I'll think of thee
when I am far away.

Care for the blood of our family,
born of your mountains and restless sea.
I've only one native country
and I will always remember thee.

Island of islands, one day I'll go
beyond this world I've known.
Island of islands, one day I'll go
back to my island home.

Ronald MacEachern

B. Nagy

Warren Gordon has operated Gordon Photographic Ltd., a photographic studio and gallery, in the business district of Sydney since 1974.
He has received regional and nation recognition for his photography and his "best-selling" book "Images of Cape Breton" has been widely acclaimed.

Verses arranged throughout this book are excerpts from complete works by some very talented writers.

Headin' for Halifax *Alastair D. MacDonald*
Bramblewood Music
Waters of Iona, My Cape Breton Home,
The Cabot Trail, The Heart of a Sailor
Lillian Crewe Walsh
Oran Do Ceap Breatainn
Dan Alex MacDonald
Rise Above Folly, Land and Sea and Season
Kenzie MacNeil
The Cape Breton Lullabye *Kenneth Leslie*
Gotham City, Down in Englishtown,
Bay of St. Ann's, Home in my Harbour
Leon Dubinsky Shag Rock Sound
Song for Peace,
(Away from) The Roll of the Sea
Allister MacGillivray
Cabot Trail Music
Returning
Anne Mae MacPherson-Skinner
Sydney in the Middle of Winter, Island of Islands *Ronald MacEachern*
Working Man, Old Man *Rita MacNeil*
Big Pond Publishing
A Test of Mettle *Max MacDonald*

Photographs were created using Pentax 6x7 equipment with Vericolor, Ektachrome, and Fujichrome film.

Photographic assistants
William K. Hollohan, Michael Carroll, Dawn Monahan, Jacqui Corbett

Reproduction Prints
Erika Runstrom

Many thanks to the people who contributed to the creation of this book.
John C. MacDonald, Barry Nagy, Ralph Dillon, Ron Linden, Bev and Allister MacGillivery, Allie MacInnis, Ester Campbell, Mr. & Mrs. Ron Martell, Betty Farrell, Ed Curtis, Ron Caplan, Marcel Doucette, Paul Como

Gordon Photographic Ltd.
(Steel Town Publishing)
367 Charlotte St.
Sydney, N.S. B1P 1E1